Love, Magic & Maroon Moons

Teas & Tonics

by Stella the Poet

Love, Magic & Maroon Moons, Teas & Tonics
© 2025 Stella the Poet, Estella L. Holeman
ISBN: 978-1-966337-30-0

Cover art: "Maroon Moon", Collage, 40"x 30"
© 1993, Phoebe Beasley

First Edition, 2025

All rights reserved. No part of this publication may be reproduced, distributed, or transmitted in any form or by any means, including photocopying, recording, or other electronic or mechanical methods, without the prior written permission of the publisher, except in the case of brief quotations embodied in critical reviews and certain other noncommercial uses permitted by copyright law.

Printed in the United States of America

Edited by Chaeyong Park
Cover Design by Sage Herrin
Layout Design by Jessica S. Lin
Layour Editor by Peter Lechuga and Erica Castro

Stella

Love, Magic & Maroon Moons

Teas & Tonics

I wrote this for US...

Table of Contents

Introduction
Foreword...
- Dear Poetry — xv
- Dear Stella the Poet — xvii

Love's Call
- The Sacred Yes — 8
- How Dare I — 9
- Love Proof — 10
- Black Love — 12
- Love Lives — 13
- Many Thanks — 15
- When Love Calls — 17
- Loving is a Verb — 18
- I Used to Be... — 19
- Kindness — 21
- Cuddle and Kiss — 22
- He's a Good Man to Lean On — 23
- Good Man Leans Back In, Too — 25
- Kindness is a Character Trait — 27
- Before Death — 28
- Grand Mommy — 29
- My White Butterfly — 31
- My Wing Span — 32

Magic
- A Blessing of Thanksgiving — 41
- My Style — 42
- Black Girl Magic — 45
- 94% Strong — 47
- Dream State/2020 — 49

Unspoken	52
Home	54
Be Kind to Yourself	57
Daily Observations	59
The Child Enters a Tree	60
Life Chant	61
This is My Nice "White People" Poem	63

Maroon Moons

The African Diaspora	70
Maroon Moons	73
A Sober Salute	74
Slave Ships Called "Jesus"	76
To My Rescue	80
Longing	83
Big Mama's Kitchen	85
Whole Life Support	87
One Nation	88
Hate	91
The Origin Story	92
I Asked the Border Patrol	93
Why Old Loves Died Young	95
Madison's Gigi	96
A Better Understanding	97
Why the Weeping Willows Weep	99
Enough Already	100
Enslavement	101
Dick and Jane	102
Emotional Baggage	103
I Know New	105
Shadows Covering Light	106
Upper Limits, Hidden Flaw	107

Learning to be Grateful	108
Acknowledgments	111
Photography Credits	113

Introduction

Love, Magic & Maroon Moons continues Stella the Poet's anthology of rhythmic literary treats. Once again, she's offering a respite for soul healing. Her poetic tonics and teas provide refrains and seeds to get you through challenging times and savor heavenly moments.

Stella the Poet offers reflections of the heart, its vulnerabilities and its ancestral strengths. This book has sunrises and moonlight memories included in the "Love's Call" series.

The "Magic" tonics are mixed with mystery and her interest in life's simple pleasures. Her magical "Dream State" includes a dream lover and mystical endeavors during night visions that came true.

Emotions arising in Stella's "Maroon Moons" reflections allow her passions and compassion full breath. She is not afraid to have courageous conversations with others and herself.

This intimate collection of poetic musings and mirrors are designed as a healing balm for soul transformation.

Love leads the way. All Light ahead!

This is Stella the Poet's second book of poetry. Her first book, Truth Shots & Ida's Brew (*first edition, 2021, second edition, 2025*) was published by World Stage Press in Los Angeles, California.

Dear Poetry

Foreword
Dear Poetry,

Your style is studied, dissected, scrutinized and taught by scholars. You're measured by tone, and rhythmic meters, figurative language like metaphors. Your flow is felt, yet you're asked to fit on a checklist with spacing, cadence, symbolism, irony and couplets.

Are you full of limericks, trochees, or alliterations? Poetry, you're often compared to Poe, Shakespeare, Emerson or Dickinson.

Can you touch souls when or where it matters? Aren't you meant for insights, self-healing and provocative conversations? Are critiques of you balanced? Are you honest in the mirror?

Poetry, your foundation in America is European focused with glorified metaphorical meanings. I come from the world of Zora, Langston, Maya and Giovanni. Where do I fit in comparison? The poetry of Sonia Sanchez and Haki Mahabuti gave my world meaning.

Poetry, do you tire of being edited, abbreviated, explained, or shortened? Is your worth in sales, public relations or social acceptance?

Does not your mere appearance have virtue and value? Aren't you most content with courageous presence, not correctness or structural elegance?

Is spoken word today a hollow echo with no relevance?

Poetry, I think the multi-dimensional aspects of expression ARE your power and essence. Are you really on a secret "Save Your Own Soul Mission?" Do the masters and doctorate students in poetry have it all twisted? Poetry is when the soul speaks, isn't it? Can it compare or compete with poetry for the elite? Just askin'?
--Stella the Poet

Stella The Poet

Open Response Letter from "Poetry"

Dear Stella the Poet,

Your "soul speak" is the only guidance needed. A heart touched is the channel I bring you.

I elevate words off paper, scatter and deploy meaningful sentences and messages. Your feelings and words are the only ones that matter.

As Poetry, I move hearts in different directions. I am much more than words in a sentence. Trust who you are and offer blessings. Let go of thinking each word must be correctly in place for soul searching.

Without me life would be just one long sentence, a straight line with no curves or opposites, no commas, or contradictions, nor new paragraphs or endings.

Spoken word is the new paradigm for heart liberation. Its generation has its own language. It moves people past the intellect. It slips truth in for clarity.

"To be," because "not to be" is out of the question.

Don't let Shakespeare shake you. Status quo is your nemesis.

Keep writing and free the souls who feel you. I am for you, not against you, regardless of what others may call poetry.

Be brave. Your experiences are unique, share them. Comparisons are impossible! You join a powerful fleet of voices.

Ignore the critics and you'll live a lot longer. Better yet, your words create new possibilities. Your books are altars for others. Your gifts will take you farther than you can imagine. Trust and hold your books sacred.

It's all in divine order. Your words are shared blessings.

Gratitude and Grace from...
 Ascended Masters, Teachers, Guides and Guardians

Love, Magic & Maroon Moons

Teas & Tonics

Love's Call

Love's Call

The opportunity to introduce this first section with Love as the theme was just too tempting. I could talk about all the different kinds of love from platonic, familial, romantic, to agape love and more. Seeing Love as omnipresent allows its grace to flow unhindered. It is laced with poems reflecting agape and community loves in my life.

Some poems here also have a romantic influence. My lover and life partner, Charles, first came to me in a dream. He didn't have a face as much as he was "a feeling". My "dream lover" met me on the beach. In my dream we ascended to heaven after a walk along the shore. As you read, you'll learn my dream became a reality three months later.

Love anchors wisdom and maturity. I offer love poems for community healing and self-reflection in this age of cynicism, skepticism and fear-based governing.

Love can be characterized as deep feelings/affection, intense emotions. To describe love as an emotional and mental state is an understatement and misunderstanding. I listened to love songs growing up. Singing to tunes with lyrics I didn't understand. It is love that brought "the birds and the bees, the flowers and the trees, the moon up above". This world can only exist as Love. It's in our heart beating and the circulation system that is carrying blood and feeding our bones. Love is the sacred essence of our human power. It's an honor to love and be loved.

I start this section with the greatest representation of Love that I know, Life! Whether it is the love of simple pleasures like moonlit nights, sharing moments with a lover, beauty in a sun's arrival or the love of children's innocence and laughter. Love rules this world. It beats the heart and wakes up the living. Love creates ways out of no way. Love is the light, the understanding known in darkness, healing communities in fear and strife.

Let's start with Life as a representation of Love. Teens in my writing classes over the years in juvenile hall, perfected an acronym for L.I.F.E. "Love Is Found Everywhere" is what they say.

As a noun/verb, Love is often described as, exciting, amazing, beautiful, powerful, electrifying, incredible, brilliant, blissful, happy, inspiring, joyous, intense, precious, spiritual, profound, wonderful, glorious, irresistible, life-changing, thrilling, breathtaking and sweet.

1 Corinthians 13:4-5, 13-13

"Love is patient, love is kind. It does not envy, it does not boast, it is not proud. It does not dishonor others, it is not self-seeking, it is not easily angered, it keeps no record of wrongs."

"And now these three remain, faith, hope and love but the greatest of these is love."

These poems will take you through the many prisms of Love. More Love and Light ahead!

This is one of my favorite quotes on love by an unknown writer...

"Being deeply loved by someone gives you strength, while loving someone deeply gives you courage."

The Sacred Yes

It's the Creator's Yes!
The Universe is for me, not against me!
The Sacred Yes! All needs are met.
The Sacred Yes to the unknown before me,
moving forward with no regrets.

It's a knowing beyond a book, a Bible, Koran or Torah.
It's a knowing beyond thoughts or actions.
The Sacred Yes is acceptance of Divine Order,
grateful for kindness and trusting blessings.

It's bearing witness to the miraculous,
like double rainbows during a rainstorm.
It's the answer when I'm doubting.
It's the answer when I'm scared.

The Sacred Yes, is evolutionary progress.
It's staying open, listening intimately,
obedient to its whispers, obedient to its calling.

With practice, the Sacred Yes
changes Living and Loving.
It helps me understand
my "no" is not a negative.
It's a knowing, teaching me
trusting is the Blessing.

This is an inspirational universe.
Creativity guides me.
All needs are met.
Despite what you may see,
It's the promise kept.

We're Living the Sacred Yes.

How Dare I

How dare I BE the love of my life
grateful for the blessings it offers.
How dare I LOVE deeply and grow
in wisdom trusting Source and Divine Order.
How dare I SEE myself as capable
and worthy without an audience for validation.
How dare I KNOW I can trust
the unknown and take magical journeys.
How dare I put myself first walking in faith, grace and courage.
How dare I LOVE, live in joy, creativity,
guided by ascended ancestors and guardian angels.

How dare I not? How dare I not be my own hero
and embrace the Divine as my mirror.
How dare I not hold you sacred, trusting
the Creator who made us.
You also radiate beauty
with perfection's permission.
I'm living in the now and enjoying every second.
I am Love, Share Love, Bathe in Love,
Wash my face in Love and spread it all over!!!
Each next moment is a blessing. I am Grateful.

Love Proof

Inspired by Rev. Dr. Clara 'Ma" Mosley on her 80th Birthday (2023)

The proof of Spirit, is Love.
Love's fruit is joy, its offspring, hope and trust.
"Patience is worth it," is what Love teaches us.
Love's kindness is generous and contagious
it grows through us.
Love's proof is the "we",
collective consciousness creating our own reality.
The Creator's Trustees,
with ancestral wisdom flowing freely.
Love speaks...
the poet's harmonies, the sculptor's ingenuity,
the painter's color palette,
the Light in a child's eye, her laughter
invoking healing possibilities.
Love's proof is nature's beauty.
We are one-of-a-kind, yet the same, holy beings,
unlike anyone or anything you've ever seen.
Those lips and hips, muscles and biceps,
those eyes, that nose, those colorful tones.
Your soul's authenticity is beauty beyond skin and bones.
You are rare and truly unique.

Like spring flowers, ancient Sequoia trees,
oceans flowing together with ease,
the clear mist, the impression on others is what's left.
You don't have to wait to be invisible,
for your Spirit to find peace.
For more Love proof, ignite your intuition and imagination.
Dream!

You're here regardless of any situation.
Look up, feel the warmth of the sun,
see the stars and the moon encased in black velvet,
sense the far away galaxies.
Love is the majesty of each season's blessings.
Find Love in the mirror.
I can see me in you.
Deep breaths make hearts open.
You are proof of Love's Intelligence.
Taken with an inhale,
your breath is pure physiological magic.
Even fake smiles help your immune system!

Love proof is always present, right here.

Black Love

On any day, Black Love is greater than white hate.
It's bigger than ignorance, fears,
illusions of privilege or political debates.
It's bigger than chaos or confusion;
it can't be lynched or erased.
It's a kind of Love steeped in the universal,
the eternity of Divinity,
the ethereal, internal, sacred and holy.
It's in the living and will never be dead.
It thrives to extinguish hatred; its Love is that bright.
It's planted in ancestral gardens.
We are its afterlife, its fruits with blossoms.
It's unshakable and unafraid.
Love's immortality laughs at death.
It's the light at the end of the tunnel.
It embraces the "ALL" good in life.
It's what is pure, what is sure about truth.
It shines through the shade and shadows.
It's the baptism in the birthing process
first human female born on African soil.

Black Love is "Ubuntu," "Camagu"
and "Yes! I AM."
Honoring the Divinity
Anointed by the Creator.   Love is bigger than Hate.

Love Lives

The sun loves living, warming us each day.
Strangers' loving glances are for human exchange.
Silence is how we communicate,
sometimes.

We recite prayers when
we're afraid. We soak in
their radiance sleeping
and awake.
The elders remind us, live long enough
to understand there are NO mistakes.

Love lives as the earth's rotation,
holding us in place.
The gift of gravity,
makes us atmospheric with grace.
Love lives for the flow of joy,
laughter, the innocence of children at play.
Wisdom says emotional pain has purpose.
Love is the reason we endure it, some say.

Loving is the commitment of life's
blood flow through our veins.
Accept what you know.
Receive the blessings of its offerings.

Welcome the Light with darkness.
Before our first breath and upon the last one,
The sweetness in the sunset and daybreak

can be a release from grief and sorrow.

Rest in peace nightly, grateful for the day.
Love living as you, having the last say.
Loving self unconditionally in a new way.
With or without perfection, or
wealth beyond measure,
loving is the only reality that matters.

It lives in the air and space.
We exist for its presence.
We're the great experiment.
It's the Soul's gift,
it's the Soul's Blessing.

Many Thanks

Grateful to the Supreme Being,
the Overseer of All Things.
Love is the Soul sourced as the Light,
it's the Guiding Force of Creativity.

Grateful for the Brightness in Brilliance,
ushering pathways through darkness.
A toast, a tea, a tonic,
to appreciation and promise.

Grateful for ancestral attendance,
perseverance and resilience,
inner Knower anointing the Highway.

A-man, A-woman, Ase,
Brothers and Sisters,
a new world order.
Evolution is rooting for us.
Fortitude leads the way.

We're here to thrive together, check joy fuel daily.
Serve self-love maintenance in a holy way.
Grateful for each day.

Sam Wilhite & Mammy Susie of Lawton Oklahoma

When Love Calls

Secret, sensual, golden pleasures,
tongue exploring sacred treasures,
eyes twinkling, fingers dancing,
the warmest chills, felt to the bone.
It's my face held in his hands, loving his
lips, embracing grace and offerings.

When love calls,
it's the sweet, the tender,
the touch that remembers,
the embers of a flame,
the Soul's promise of forever.
It's in the heart of surrender,
the joy of "just between us" laughter.
It's in the breathless pause,
the spark of possibilities,
making love in beauty and timeless space.
It's life transforming,
a sacred event
ushering a richer togetherness,
when Love calls my name.

Loving is a Verb

Timeless memories,
instinctive giving,
grace with ease,
cherished blessings,
a trusted friend.

When Love calls
it's in tonal cadence
ancient timbers,
syncopated rhythms,
harmonized breathing,
synchronized living.

It's the sound of seagulls departing,
ocean waves with moonlit waltzes.
It's in the sun's shine and a star's light,
faint whispers in the wind. It is
Higher Consciousness calling,
it's a new beginning.

It's Soul transformation time
when Love Calls my name.

I Used to Be...

I used to be a slave, but now I'm free,
lost the shackles of limited thinking.
Free for healing, envisioning children thriving,
growing up safely in this land of the free.

Free to think about when Palestine is free.
When genocide is no longer seasonal.
Free to imagine peace and not screams.
Free to imagine when Arabs
stop trafficking human beings.
When Christians, Muslims and Jews are
no longer persecuted for their religions.
When religious zealots accept we are all free.

Free to envision when Mother Africa
benefits from her own rich minerals.
Free to think about famine ending in the Congo
and the Sudan, people no longer starving, when
the unsheltered can get on their feet.

I used to be shy but now I speak up,
I use my poetic voice to uphold women's rights and social justice.
I used to be afraid but now
I stand courageously with ancient freedom fighters,
packs of runaway slaves,
and poets speaking truth to power.

Releasing fears, diving in deep
swimming through currents with grace and ease.

Floating on my back, kissing the sun,
looking up at the stars, the inner Light my guidance.

My hope lives in the flickers of prayer candles.
It comes from sparks in warm fires and kind thoughts.
I used to be mad a lot. Now, I live in peace more often.

This is more than a poem, it's an honest assessment.
We don't have to be haters when loving feels so tender.
There is a "One Love" solution. Look in the mirror.
It's the perfect place to start.

I used to be blind but now I see
strangers' eyes smiling, hearts opening.
I even see more folks hugging trees.

What did you use to be?

Kindness

Kindness.
It's in the light in his eyes,
the joy in his laughter.
It's in the way he pulls me in,
his loving embrace holding me in place.
It's when, with a boyish grin,
he tilts his head and calls me "baby."
Kindness is felt and not questioned.
It feels authentic when offered and
healing when accepted.
It can't be sold, yet if traded
on the open market its
value is more than gold.
Kindness witnessed
is wealth rendered,
it's a natural trait offered from a
well of abundance and strength. Try some of it.
We are all richer for it, I promise.

Cuddle and Kiss

Pleasing you makes me happy.
I love to cuddle and kiss
squeeze and tease
as you rub my back
and stroke my neck.
I love my feet rubbed
my head caressed,
my lips warmed and welcomed.
I love to look in your eyes,
laugh loud, throw back my head,
sway my hips, smile and slow dance.
I love synchronized releases and fast explosions.
Asleep, I feel your body
next to mine, the tender parts need what you offer.
Grateful for the gift of you…
Affirming my appetite and offering
reassurance, "So, so satisfied"
is my new chant.
"Yes, thank you, more please" is my new mantra.

He's a Good Man to Lean On

A good man to lean on,
strong and sturdy like the
African walking staff.
His strength is seen
yet invisible,
it's how we love, it's how we fit.
His arms are my sanctuary,
he catches me before I fall,
He restores my faith in my abilities.
Our sweet love making, a tantric flow.
Together we're the header
between columns
we stand together,
yet alone.
We're the arch in the trees
forming canopies,
we're black wood
in ancient groves.
Like the mustard seed
nurtured by the sun,
he's the mighty oak
sculpted by God.
Like the ancient Sequoia
trees, his shade is my refuge,
his nature kind and caring.
Like an echo from the mountaintop,
he feels like my father's heart,
pure, protective, Loving.
It's a sacred acquaintance,
a dream fulfilled.
Alone is never lonely,

ROBERT L. HOLEMAN

grateful to be fulfilled,
"there's the world,"
but first, "there's us."

Opening the eye
between my legs,
I'm receiving appreciation,
Goodness, and finding trust.
Learned asking the right question is an art.
One day I asked the universe
"Show me how men love me"
found the answer soon thereafter.
A good man offers love,
peace, shares resources and blessings.
If naked and
cold, with honor, you are the cover.
Grateful for strength,
vulnerability and the mystic love of the ancestors
make leaning time
a privilege and an honor.

In general, good men to lean on...
They are gifts from Love.
Whether you are a
father, brother, friend or
lover,
you are shelter. We're
stronger knowing, when necessary,
we're here for each other.

Just wanted to say...Thank You.

Good Man Leans Back In, Too...

A good man to lean on,
is a wonderful way
to recline, a happily ever-after.
It's a warm hug lasting forever.
He's a wish come true,
becoming so satisfied,
feels old, exciting and new.
With a sweet smile
good man leans in too,
tree trunk firmly planted,
eyes offer deep penetration
he holds me firm, yet tender.
Good man to lean on keeps me
limber, massages my bark,
softens my edges.
He satisfies my soul,
supports breath and
branch extensions,
He makes me fearless and courageous.
His wish is my pleasure.
He holds me with grace and honor.
Grateful for his Love and Kindness.
I am stronger knowing
we're here for each other.

Good men are a Blessing
to love and know.
They sparkle like diamonds
and are rare to behold.

Good men, I believe in you.
Your presence on earth
makes me smile all over.
I know some good women looking for a
good man to lean back in, too.
If you fit this description,
smile with that twinkle in your eye,
send her a signal.
You're strong and sturdy, too!

Kindness is a Character Trait

Kindness...
The kinship of Spirits,
the surrender of old stories,
a communion with angels,
self-forgiveness again and again.

Self-acceptance without judgment
is the source for self-loving.
Kindness is the feeling of freedom.
It's the cool breeze on a hot summer day.
It's answered prayers again and again.
Kindness returned is divine order
and loving compassion.
It's the healing of cancer,
the vaccination that works,
it's Grace under fire,
a stranger's thoughtful gesture.
It's what makes us human.

Kindness is the promise to
"rest in peace,"
before dying.

Now is the time
to hold yourself
in a sacred way.
Kindness is the wisdom.
Knowing right now,
these are courageous, holy days.

Before Death

Before death we live.
We live the last moments
faithful in the exit.
We came to leave,
it's the kept promise
upon first breath.
It's about what we do in-between
the beginning and ending dash.
It is Love as Divinity Rising....
Cosmic energy flowing through
from the depths of my being.

The promise from Life's beginning?

We are held in Love.

Grand Mommy

Alice Ligon, an ancient loving being.
My Grandmother—me, a grandchild,
her sacred heart recipient from the start.
She modeled Love for me.
Proud indigenous Choctaw roots,
blue eyes, white skin. Had a half French/black father.
Her Mother, full blooded native American.
When I was young, Grandmommy let us brush
her long black straight hair growing down her back.
She loved her four "colored" grandchildren from the start
with all her heart.

Considered an old maid at twenty-five,
she married the darkest man she could find.
He married the closest woman he could find to might,
never heard Love mentioned among them.
Their guide was their marriage vows.
She was born July 4, 1904
in Natchez, Mississippi, one of five.
One observation of mine?
She always brought plates to the men
waiting at the dinner table,
the girls had to fend for themselves.
A generation in the land of the free
at the turn of the century.
She registered "colored" voters
and taught folks how to read.
She didn't let others
define who she would be as a

mixed race woman with
a seventh-grade education.
In the silence she prayed
and read the L.A. Times daily.
Not sure if she knew the implications
of proudly naming my Daddy after the
Confederate general Robert E. Lee!
Daddy never mentioned the origin of his name.
He just walked precincts making sure
Black folks got to the polls to vote
in the nineteen fifties
and sixties
by any means necessary.

My White Butterfly

She's my white butterfly.
Now, she's my heart with wings.
Walking out my front door
she flutters in my
face to greet me.
The moment I saw her I
knew she was a Blessing
from the heavenly skies,
Grandmommy, my Daddy's
Mother, is my white butterfly.

My Wingspan

Wings spread wide open, trusting the beauty surrounding me...the refined art, the crystal palace, an inheritance of creative possibilities. Travels to faraway lands and the custom built home I'm found in, the extended family, the love of strangers, the wealth of intimate love,
Godchildren and
family-friends.

My wings extend, fully embracing me, my wings flutter and fly landing on my own agency. Trusting self-care, words of sacred truths holding me. Wings internally lined with magical tools, healing energy flowing through me. With focus and clarity, the inner knower responds to living and loving intuitively.

A seed line, giving birth to new landscape, new territory, feeding me. Wingspan gliding and soaring connecting to multi-dimensional ancestry. Teaching, caring, loving guidance anchored by the North Star and humanity. I live in eternity. I know Love. Divinity is Love's Journey.
I trust.
I am Blessed and Deserving.

Today I look up, I look out. Mental strength and emotional well-being are my wealth, with or without a body.
I fly free!

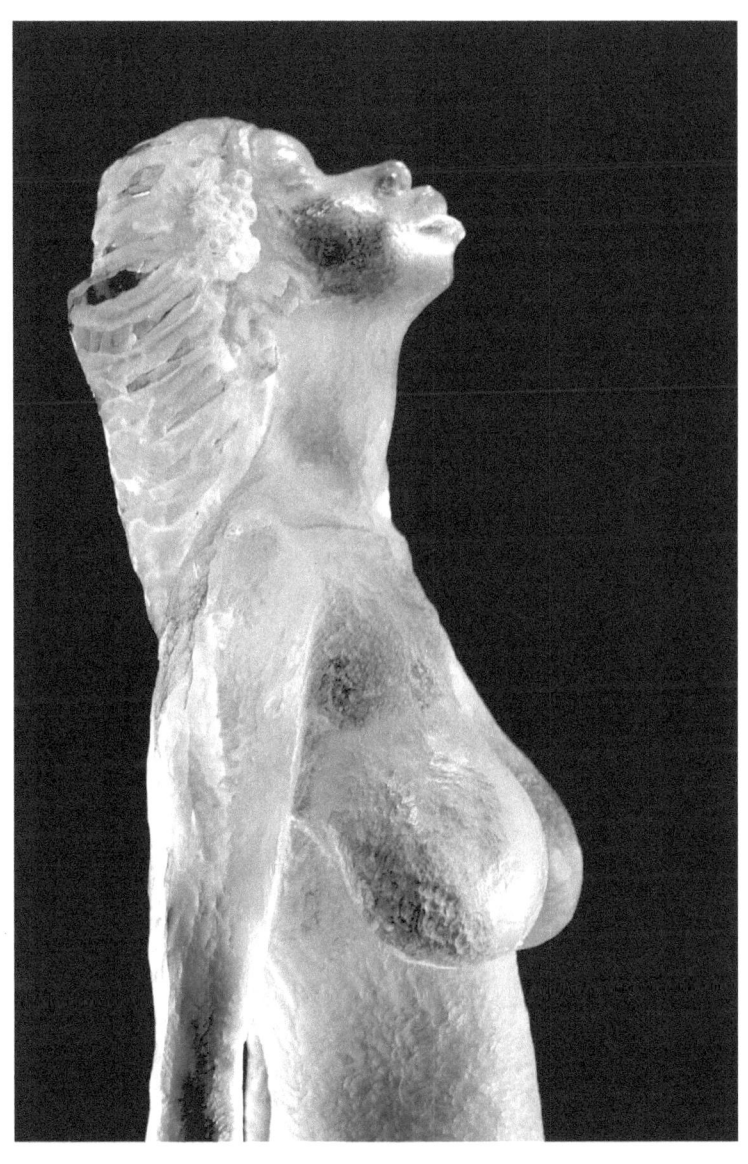

"Surrender" hand-carved acrylic by Charles Dickson

Magic

Magic

A definition of magic is "the power of apparently influencing the course of events by using mysterious or supernatural forces." We are not magic. We are magical.

In the beginning God created the heaven and the earth. 2 And the earth was without form, and void; and darkness was upon the face of the deep. And the Spirit of God moved upon the face of the waters. 3 And God said, Let there be light; and there was light. Genesis 1:1-3 (KJV)

Light/Life is amazing and magical when you stop and think about it. Just the miracle of your birth is cloaked in mystery to the time, place and evolution of the seed planted. Life itself is miraculous.

Magical. Its appearance is "unbelievable." For instance it "appears" like you could not "imagine" how "something" just took place "right in front of your eyes." It's wonderment, synchronicity, flow, divine order, serendipity, passionate purpose made possible, need met instantly, the manifestation of the impossible all at the same time.

No part of our bodies, minds or hearts did we consciously make. Not one cell, organ, hair follicle, beat of the heart or breath did we construct, plan or make a concerted effort to create. Human beings did not create the human form, its lifetime, or anything that drives it.

In 2023, as we began to talk about artificial intelligence replacing human beings, let's remember, the first word of that construct, "artificial." Anything that does not derive from an original source can be considered artificial, inauthentic, a fake, a fraud and/or a manipulation of what is real. Source energy is wholeness, completeness, fullness. Its origin is what makes it real.

The magic referred to in these pages reflects the supreme authority, authenticity, the truth of the substance behind the substance and appearance. The source is the force field activating the synchronicity of life, the joy of met needs and answered prayers. This magic has special keys creating magical dreams, manifestations, and healing happenings with grace preceding outcomes. "The way 'in' is the way out," my friend, songwriter/vocalist, Rickie Byars, sings.

Inspired by a chapter in one of Judy Hall's Crystals to Inspire You, magic has many levels and ways to access its authority. These are portals that usher in magic.
- Believe in Yourself
- Follow your Passions
- Invest in Your heart's desires
- Use the power of Imagination

These are my lucky charms. Also, giving away something that you value is the first step in manifesting abundance and inviting blessings. The womb of creation is the cauldron of magic. An incantation of possibilities realized, "a grateful heart" are in the power and source of the being activating magic.

It's divine order that "Magic" follows the section on "Love" in this book. Love has a magic of its own. Magic is introduced by Love because what else can you call magic? Love in the blood flowing through your body, the gifts of veins and arteries, your ability to hear and see. Feel how much magic and joy comes from love's motivating, inspiring, passionate desire fueled by creative drive and clarity to be of service and make a difference.

Magic is combustion, the spark plug, the intuitive connection putting you in the right place at the right time. Magical is the man in my life. My soul mate who has always been my friend. Becoming intimate late in life, we connected during a fire and lockdown in Compton on the day I brought him a copy of my first book, *Truth Shots & Ida's Brew*. He had donated some photos of artwork to it. I wanted to thank him, drop off a book and get out of Compton before dark. But there was a greater plan.

What I didn't know was that I had dreamed about someone like him and wrote a poem about it three months earlier. He is part of the poem "Dream State" that follows these pages. What was going to be a brief trip turned out to be a lifetime adventure now, with the man I love. I dreamed about him long before I knew who "he" was.

The magic of dreams, the guidance of reassurance. My dream offerings are truly magical. When I asked the universe for a "traveling companion" in my friend Laura Day's (author of Practical Intuition) workshop the summer of 2020, I knew he was on his way by December that year. I kept telling my friend, Ashley, that someone "familiar" was coming into my life. I had no idea it would be an old friend whose lovely wife, Darlene, had passed away! Faith and Love are essential ingredients for activation of magic.

Wonderment is God's plan and pleasure.

The Universe is Magical. The stars, planets, moons, the flow of the ocean, the birth, death, the honoring of Loved Ones, the darkness, the depth, the silence, the cry of a newborn. That's all Magic.

What is magical as human evidence? The unexplainable, the part that has no real logic or sequence, the unexpected, the mystical. Magic is life's alchemy.

This section is about what is magical in life. The thoughts that become dreams. The mystical aspects of coincidence, divine order, the healings from a dimension of grace and humility.

There are "magical" words in the English language. They are known as "switch words." The origin of switch words are taken from the magic formulas in the tale of "Ali Baba and the Forty Thieves."

Switch words are rooted in "open sesame." It's said there are certain words that bypass the conscious mind and goes straight to the subconscious for activation. Words have power.

Switch words are modern mantras. They are divine blessings in their purest sense. They have the ability to quickly switch your energy from one dimension to another.

"Divine Order, Together and Done" are a few examples of switch words that instantly shift energy. Research says that if I am suffering from pain and want relief, the word to say is "change." To achieve mastery in something, the switch word is "together." The switch word functions as an electric switch. The brain goes on auto pilot for action.

Words are magical. We use them as evidence of life's mysteries revealed.

Together.

Done.

A Blessing of Thanks-Giving

What is kindness
when the world feels cruel and hateful?
A blessing of Thanksgiving,
feeling grateful, being the Light in the dark,
grasping for hope and finding it.
Daring to love each other, clearing the air.
It's commitment to self-care.
Kindness is a flash of brilliance,
a revolutionary, contagious act!
It has a rippling impact.
It's a word that starts with "K"
but always ends with more loving.
It's rooted in the sun,
it crystallized the earth,
it's in the moon's reflection,
the twinkle in the stars,
the fire's warmth and glow.
It's spring's inheritance with winter's snow.
Kindness is humanity's promise to strangers.
Being humane matters. It's never overrated.
Kindness is essential for human growth.
It's heart magic.   Heart magic rules the world.

My Style

My style is rhythmic.
I hear it in my heartbeat.
It moves like poetry,
the flow of the wind,
the cool breeze in the air
on July days.
My style sings songs.
It plays instruments with my tongue,
its harmonies, its beats,
its melodic tones, it keeps its alignment
with the sun, the moon, the galaxies.
It's grace. My style is the silence between the lines.
My style is prayers in poems heard often.
My style sparks fires, it reshuffles the deck,
it can be a tornado, smoldering embers,
it's a loud laugh, a quiet smile, a fragile tear,
compassion facing truth
showing people, I love, I care.
It's courage to face my fears.
Its strength beyond awareness.
My style is long form and instrumental.
It's cursive and three-dimensional doodling.
It can be a loud laugh or
the last word you never heard.
My style is jazz and free form.

From left to right, "Aunt Janice, E. Wong, Lucille and Aunt Hazel

Estella

Very fashionable c̄ all these hair styles on this page.

Black Girl Magic

Glad I was born a Black Girl.
Grew up dancin'
to rhythm and blues
and eating soul food, Southern style.
Family meals were greens, cornbread, fried chicken
and sweet potato pie. Always had fish on Fridays
and spaghetti with meatballs weekly.

My life was Stevie Wonder rich
framed in Motown-music memories.

Michael was a Jackson Five singing about his ABC's.
Marvin Gaye offered sexual healing.
Luther Vandross was a slow grind
and I danced to Queen Aretha with respect.

Hanging out now, "Auntie" has a sexy sixties gray crown,
my ponytail sparkles with love locs on my head.
I am happy and nappy with my mohawk.
Proud of Black girl magic to this day.

History and pride affirm my presence.
Black girl magic is innocence in
numbers, fireside chats with youngsters,
Aunties sharing experiences.
Black girl magic is comfort with
Sisters/friends who have your back to this day.

My hips are pork chop plump,
my lips, full and luscious.
My rhythm is natural and organic.
Light-years are in my bounce.
I bow to my sisters with natural heads
and praise God-given bodies.
Black girl magic recognizes ancestral inheritance.

Truth is not at war with itself.

I laugh with glitter; I rock to ancient drums.
Most people in the world are of color.
So, wherever I go, I am home.

Black girl magic keeps me strong.

Grandmammy Louise

94% Strong

Black Women
standing their ground
having their say,
moving in harmony in
a sacred way.
94% strong,
undeterred, unblemished
future focus
I am grateful to know
we have friends, lovers
and each other.
One God, Third Eye Vision,
onward my Sistahs, a standing ovation.
Our mission is to continue to love and
protect one another.
No matter the battle, the war,
the appearance of an ending,
we are the medicine, we heal
in community.

Take your time. Be gentle with yourself.

Communing in nature and beauty
renews a fearless Force
anointed by the Creator.
We live for children dreaming
of safer harbors.
We're the Lighthouse
for unpredictable tomorrows.
Believing in a world where
loving each other will be sustained,
where innocence and hope can play together.
A place where safety is no longer
the price we pay for the laborious truth
of America's sins.

94% strong Black Women
voting in mass in America in 2024!
There's no loss, only gain.
When we look in the mirror,
pride and purpose make it
worth it again and again.
Sisterhood makes it easier
to sleep at night these days.
We cuddle with our community
and like the neighbors we've made.

What about you, U.S. Citizen
who voted in the cruelty being inflicted?
Hallucinations have a price.
Hope you like your reflection in the mirror.

94% strong only get stronger and stronger.

Dream State/2020

I had a dream last night
about a stranger who loves me.
His eyes told me I was
the most beautiful woman
he'd ever seen.
It was a new relationship.
Mentioning his first wife
but making it quick.
Big, beautiful brown,
tall, Brother.
He had strong limbs, a big puffy afro on his chin,
clear brown eyes, and a big shy grin.
First touching my arms,
with his shy smile at first,
we were soon naked together
quenching our thirst.
Time was sweet.
It stood still it seemed.
He played with my hair,
stroked my body gently,
before applying his Light beam.
At first, he dared to see.
Is his touch welcomed?
I smiled and closed my eyes
opening myself to heaven.
We moved slowly in motion.
Becoming One,
we disappeared in Light
immersed

in sacred devotion.
Later we passed the beach
on the walk back to my suite.
Feeling love and excitement
brewing inside of me.
Almost forgot about
the dream this morning.
He was Tootsie Roll brown,
tall, fine, thoughtful,
sweet, strong and all mine.
He lifted me up, floating like a feather,
in heaven with him was all that mattered.
I smile now, from the inside out,
all cells fired up remembering the
immersion in Light.
I returned to this world
toes curled, with smiles lit bright
every time I remember
beaming in Love and Light.
Asking Spirit for an answer
the reply was simple.
Trust what you feel
in order to heal.
Love is Supreme.
Trust its Light.
Trust its Power.

So, I sleep tonight
awaiting the dreamer's hour.
Thinking about my dream lover,
elevating me like no other.

Stillness reigns anticipating
the firing of inner lights
in the heavenly halls of this dreamer's
delights!

Unspoken

She's the Rainbow Serpent
She will NOT go Unspoken.
Ethereal, mystical, quiet radiance,
timeless beauty beyond skin and bones.
Grace and dignity unfiltered,
nurturing breast and arms are home.

In the eye of the beholder,
Behold beauty, Divine Order.
First earth woman, sacred structure,
brave, intuitive, ancient messenger
whispers "trust Love and Know."

Sculpted organic elegance, fearless.
Bold, Goddess, Divine Mother,
wholeness, completion,
unclothed, uncovered, unbroken.
Creator's Womb-man,
carrier of human potential,
humanity heals in her arms.
She's the Rainbow Serpent

She will not go Unspoken....

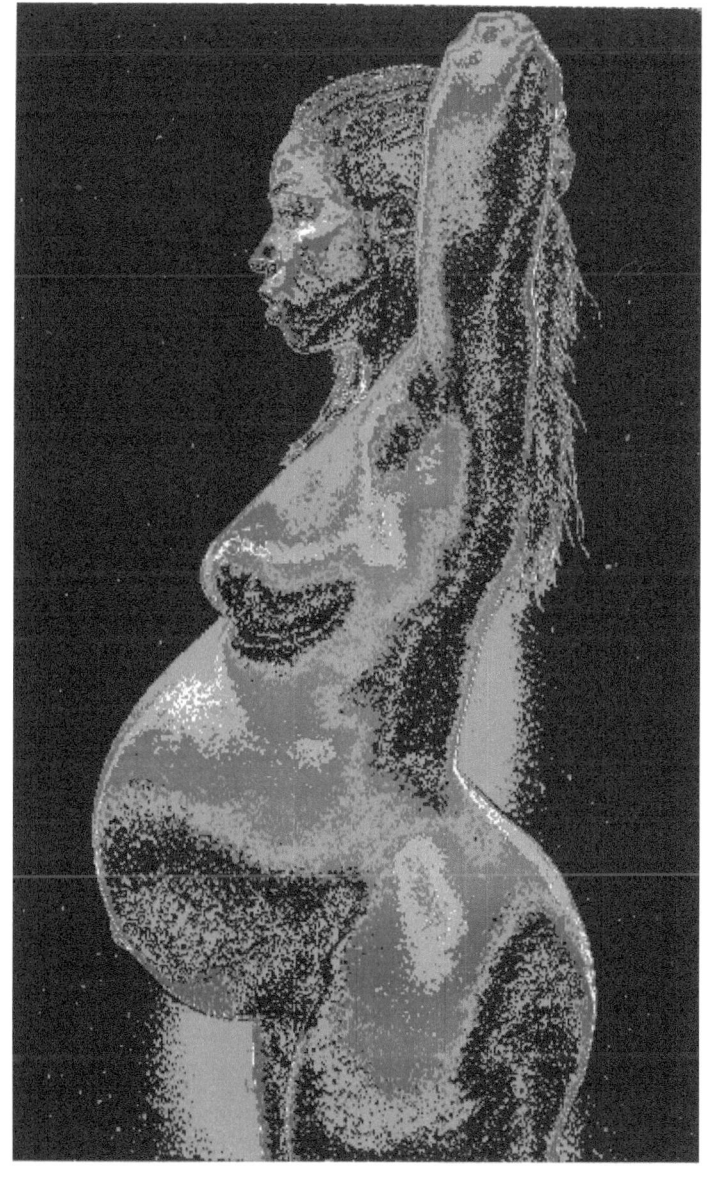

Home

Home is a loving feeling.
The feeling of safety,
the warmth of aromas
in the morning
like coffee, bacon and eggs.
The comfort of eating homemade
peach cobbler and ice cream.
It's knowing someone cares.

It tastes like the
sweet nectar of ripe
persimmons, it's a natural feeling
like amber oozing from an apricot tree.
Home is the residue left in the
hives of the honeybees for tasting.

It's remembering the taste of sweet potato pie
and a cool breeze on summer evenings.

Home is the memories of
Grandma's annual visits,
her bedtime songs
like "Baa Baa, Black Sheep."
Home is the pat on the back,
the rub on the head,
the found treasure,
the cooling salve in aloe vera,
an African violet's completion in full bloom.
It's a deep breath seeing natural
beauty like the Sequoia trees or mountains in Sedona.
Home within feels like children's laughter,
innocence and joy, happiness beyond measure.
Nature held sacred.
Home feels like soul satisfaction
after a creative endeavor.
It's the inner Light's reflections.
Home is a safe place to surrender with a smile.
Wherever Love is…. Home is there.
It's peace of mind,
a long deep breath of surrender!
It's not made from walls or materials.
It's the feeling you're loved unconditionally.
Home is the place where Light lives.
It's portable and mobile.
It's where vulnerability is honored.
It's the touch of a healer, the embrace of a lover,
self-acceptance or the advice of a trusted friend.

Home is a healing tone that echoes
"All your needs are met whether you see
it or not," where there is breath there's hope,
dreams turn into memories stored in your Soul.
Home is where magic lives.
Home is inside. Home is here...

Be Kind to Yourself

Be kind to yourself.
Don't carry
what doesn't serve you.
Let go and shake it off.
A kind act is loving yourself
regardless of what is taken or overlooked.
Kindness breeds more loving deeds.

Say "Hello beautiful" with
a smile in the mirror.
Be tender with yourself.
It's a love tonic that's complete.
Lean into fear, it's information.

Is it "false evidence appearing real" fear
or "forget everything and run?" fear
Only you know.
Be the gratitude you want to receive.
Protecting yourself is loving.
Most of all, be kind and caring,
let it reflect in the mirror.
Healing takes time.
It can't be done in a hurry.
We are worthy
of kindness and so much more.
Are you ready
to receive your own loving?
Find a way for it to flow easily.
Know it starts
with you but touches all of us,
bearing witness to your presence
on this earth....

Daily Observations

I bend but do not break.
I am warmed by the daily sun.
I raise my head, yet bow to deep roots.
The earth my sanctuary, sky my refuge.
I keep my promise to wake daily.
I find balance after fierce winds.
The noon hour reminds me the day is not over.
The evening shade renews a center
encouraging relaxation and slumber.
I rest in darkness with my dream lovers,
extended branches protect me as cover.
Internal rings of fire hold me in place.
I am the mighty oak tree. I was the mustard seed's promise.
My purpose in life is loving.
I offer breath and shade.
I provide oxygen.
My gift is faith and presence.

Lean on me. I am always here just for you.

The Child Enters a Tree
(from a class with author, Dorothy Randall Gray)

The child enters the ancient tree in the forest
to feel her center.
She enters the womb of creation, the cavity of a living Sequoia
sculpture.
She's cradled in a surrounding that's holy, an opening.
The child walks in slowly, unafraid.
She's a faith-walker entering into a wholeness that's sacred.
A tree for healing, she enters knowing protection.
It's the form God is taking all because a child enters the
unknown.
A re-awakening, grounded in everything "divinity," a
remembrance, an embrace of its maker, rooted in a love haven.
When a child enters a tree it's a recalibration
of trusting and knowing.
She enters surrendering. She's hugged by pure peace.

Life Chant

We came here leaving,
it's the kept promise
for the gift of life's magic.
Loving done in-between is
your Divinity Rising.
"Divine energy flowing through me
from the depth of my being.
Held in love from Life's beginning,"
is my decree to live it out fully.
Before "so-called" death
living is our existence.
Living each moment
faithfully, as a gift,
like a proud
promise kept.

Amen.

"Wishing on a Star", public art sculpture by Charles Dickson in front of the California African American Museum in Los Angeles

This is My Nice "White People" Poem

Nice white people...
Those are the ones who grew up in my neighborhood.
The ones who hung out at parties and marry into the family.
They were a part of us, the ones who took the bus.
The neighbors whose children
gather and play and feel like kin on holidays.
Nice white people...
Not a part of the middle passage.
It's those who hid our ancestors
helped free them, the abolitionists, the African diaspora kin.
If there were white heroes during slavery, I'm talkin' about them.
Nice white people....
like the ones who took a beating, or the
comrades murdered by the KKK in 1964.
The ones pulled from a bus protesting
segregation in Mississippi.
John Goodman's friends,
Schwerner and Chaney.
Nice White People...
They recognize humanity, want to be an instrument
for balancing insanity, understand stop and frisk
in New York City was always wrong.
They are the ones who took a knee, sing the gospel,
credit my race and rehearse freedom songs.
Nice White People...
They smile for no reason,
ask if they can help and unapologetically
stand beside others in truth, liberty and justice for all.
Nice White People...

Believe in humanity and human dignity throughout the ages.
They, too, believe human beings don't belong in cages.
Nice White People have more in common with me than
strangers.
Some are just really good human beings.
The ones like Edith Jacobs
who loaned my Godmother E. Wong
money without any questions.
Edith's son, became E. Wong's Godson too,
so she could protect him from
a Black stepfather's physical abuse.

Some White bodies have deeper roots.
They are loving, kind, and caring.
They are like the ones who looked like my
grandmother, Alice, and her siblings in Natchez, Mississippi.
She was born July 4, 1904,
with French and Choctaw Indian roots.
She had long, straight black hair,
until it turned white and flowed down her back.
She had blue eyes and white skin.
This is where my
Nice White People Poem ends and begins.
My grandmother makes me pause, stand in truth.
Not root for nice white people, but
just root for good human beings.
May change this poem's title to
"good human beings come
in all colors."
My grandmother was key in
filling my life up with pure,
unconditional Loving.

CITY OF ANGELS
SCIENCE OF MIND CENTER

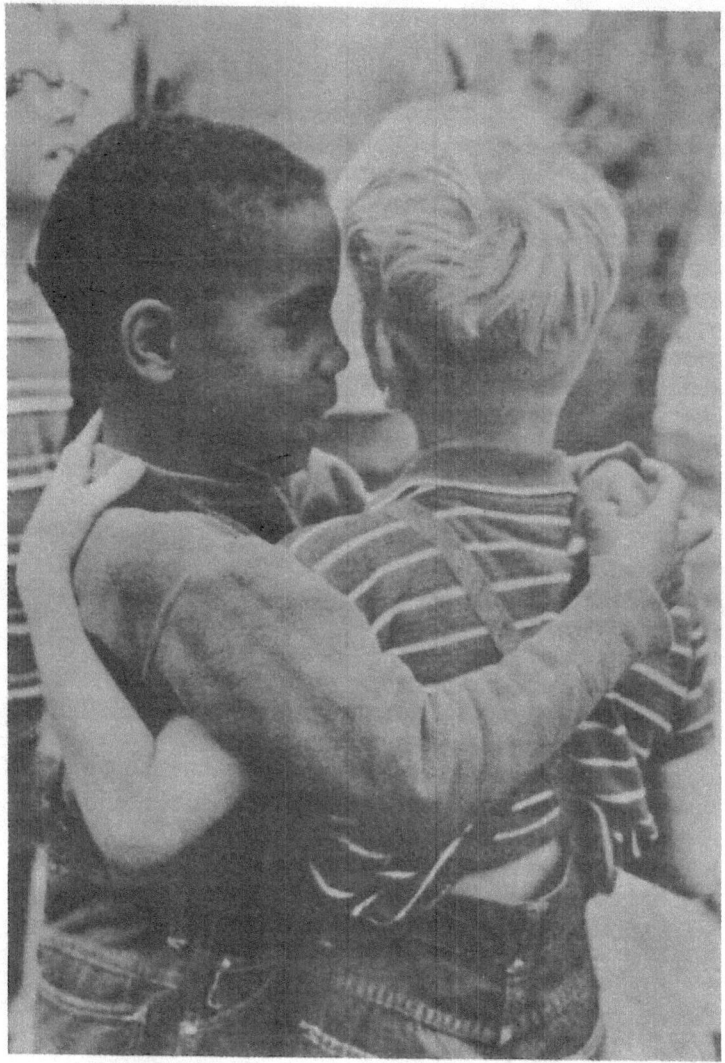

LET'S MAKE THIS WORLD
A BETTER PLACE FOR YOU AND ME

Maroon Moons

Maroon Moons

Honoring my heroes: the women, the men, the children whose work heals and touches others. Honoring those who help us to self-understand, self-correct and fortify ourselves.

This section offers soulful motivation and poetic meditations. It's for the heart feeling, eyes seeing and ears hearing between poetic lifelines. I can name her, or him, from recent bright light poets like Amanda Gorman to June Jordan to Sonia Sanchez and so many others who inspire my writing. Love me my legendary greats Gwendolyn Brooks, Langston Hughes, Haki Mahabuti, Nikki Giovanni and Maya Angelou. I am inspired by spiritual mentors like Ida B. Wells Barnett, Harriet Tubman and Sojourner Truth. My first book of poetry, Truth Shots & Ida's Brew pays tribute to them.

I'm inspired by the writers of the Anansi Writer's Workshop led by V. Kali at the World Stage in Los Angeles. It's been in Leimert Park for more than thirty years. When my moons look maroon, I know there are always others feeling it too on a Wednesday night in the Black community of spoken word artists. Brother Kamauu Daaood, legendary-wordsmith, co-founded the institution.

But what is a poetic hero but a voice in the dark, illuminating with works and deeds, the spark of the heart, the rhythm with the rhyme, the healing of words repeated in time, a hero's offering taking us places we need to go, if only to save our own soul? My heroes, my favorite poets, leave an undeniable impression. They are a growing army of truth crusaders, rebel rousers, wordsmiths extraordinaire, a timeless infusion of wisdom.

My friend, Phoebe Beasley's, work is on the cover of this book. Her original artwork is called Maroon Moon. That title inspired the section you are about to read.

These glimpses of Maroon Moons leaves their scent in the air.

The African Diaspora

Migrants...First Born Earth Beings
baptized by dandelion sprays.
The Chosen, soaked in sun
seeds planted in the ocean's mud.

Africa answered the earth's
first human calling, her
frequency felt around the world.
Kind hearts the native tongue.
In praise and kinship,
I am here.

Miraculous in flesh on humble knees
I am here in literary writings from Fanon
to Angelou, in the fine arts,
from Bakari, Hoyes, Dellis and Dickson.
From Zizipo, Andile, Zanele and Terence
I'm here in LA from South Africa.

The African Diaspora is borderless.
Spreading Love and Light is its natural beauty.
I am here in rhythms, the Blues and dance.
in African drums and Cuban vanguards,

I am here in samba, spirituals and jazz.

From Baptisms by Fire to
Baptisms down by the river side.
I am here, seeds buried with ocean water.

The Black humans, learning how to fly.
Inoculated from fear, bowing heads
with ancestral integrity and honor.
I am here.

With inner strength and vision
to climb the mountaintop,
secured with fortitude and courage to
move beyond blockages and hurdles.

The African Diaspora expands as Light
and germinates in darkness.
It slumbers at night, dreaming its birth in limbo.
I am here.

This earth is the altar
created to love each other
and lie peacefully with each other on it.

The Sacred's way of healing community

is remembering we stand

empowered knowing, the Black "I" is a collective force.

It knows Higher Intelligence,

spreads Love not war.

The African Diaspora, people of color,

Asia, Latin America, Indigenous natives

rule this planet by numbers.

I am a divine dandelion spray in the breeze.

I am here.

Never to be forgotten.

Maroon Moons

Loving is the gift life offers.
Immortality evolving human existence
makes Love our essence at birth.

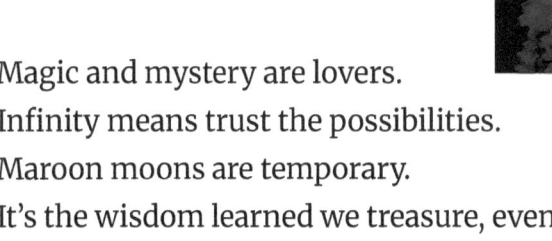

Loving life matters
regardless of its phases,
like the moon, it changes its look.

Magic and mystery are lovers.
Infinity means trust the possibilities.
Maroon moons are temporary.
It's the wisdom learned we treasure, even
when we're bleeding, trust and know.

Reflections throughout history.
Maroon Moons are burgundy
hues with subtle tones of black and gold.
They open us to Loving the wisdom in anger.
Accepting the tension in the air.

Overcoming obstacles, learning higher ground
jumping hurdles, reaching new heights, stretching in midair.

The Maroon Moon trance brings sacred orders.

If you care
about the future.
It's time to pay attention.   It's here.

A Sober Salute

A heavenly toast and sober salute to Ida's Brew with shots of
Sojourner's Truth.
Calling in ascended masters, teachers, guides and guardians.
Calling in brothers and sisters of Love and Light....
Grateful for the North Star
and whispers from angels in the dark.
Grateful for the final smell of freedom,
the wisdom in looking forward not back.
Grateful for necks that didn't crack,
backs that didn't break,
police who didn't profile,
perpetrators who had to pay,
and for the innocent who kept running and got away.
Grateful for the vigilantes that tired from chasing,
and for the guilty found guilty more often.
Grateful for police body cameras bearing witness
so communities don't feel so betrayed.
Toasting the Guardian Angels,
the Soul mentors,
the Light keepers
making sure the crude,
the rude, the insane, the ignorant,
the mean and hateful,
don't get their way.
Remembered in this salute
are the Sea Spirits,
souls of the lost, the stolen,
the neglected, the indigenous, and those who made
a way out of no way.

Divine Ones, Precious Ones
resting in peace, trusting destiny.
Grateful for protection in stormy seas.
Thankful for ancestral Loving,
for the Sunrise, the Light of the World each day.
We thrive as collective consciousness for healing.
Our DNA is organic and divinely sequenced....
My life is infused with gratitude.
This is how I pray.

Salud and Ase'

Slave Ships Called "Jesus"

A slave ship called "Jesus of Lubeck"
was the first to be anointed
by Queen Elizabeth in 1563.
Up to six-hundred African bodies
lined in the hull. It was part of
King Henry the VIII's fleet.

The British built wealth, capturing,
trading and selling, enslaved men,
women and children, millions buried at sea
while cruising the west African coast
trading guns for human beings.

By 1619, they landed in the Americas,
with a similar name for their fleet.
It was called the "Good Ship Jesus."
They tried to take Black people's
humanity away under religion.

May these words heal the
Sea Spirits, sprouting underwater branches.
On dry land the once enslaved
descendants of those trees,
African Americans.
Our ancestors' call was heard,
letting them know they've come this far,
because, "there's something greater."
They knew "Jesus" was never their savior.
But the Christ-Light was on board.

Their presence felt and whispers heard.
The "Good Ship Jesus" was named by enslavers.
The authentic name for the Christ,
is Yeshua. That's the soul saver.

Like the waves roaring and crashing,
truth when heard awakens the anointed.
It heals generational wounds and false ideologies.
Heaven and hell are of our own making.

The galaxies, suns, moons, stars,
the ravens, hummingbirds, the monarch butterflies,
the eternal life within whispers quietly in the breeze…
"Your Soul has always been free.
Any bondage held over you is a fallacy.

Free your Mind. No sinners here. Be clear.
The Divine is your breath in alignment.
You were born in My image and likeness.
You already have what's
needed. There's nothing missing. The
truth of you as my Creation can free you."

Creativity and self-loving is what
it means to be Living. Look in the mirror.
Love what you see, no pretending.
That's true power and freedom.

So take this as a warning…
"Beware of false prophets,
coming to you in sheep's

clothing"... know those who damn you
to hell in eternity, may not know how to
create heaven on earth among the living.
The Light in Darkness is the Soul Saver.

Meanwhile, if you happen to see
vessels moving on the seas
in the "Good Ship Jesus," fleet?
May I advise...? Stay alert,
take cover, look within for Yahweh
stay alert and pray with your feet!

E. Wong

To My Rescue

To my rescue...
My grandmother's visits; from Memphis.
We went to the train station to pick her up.
Every year she came to
visit, after the death of my grandfather,
she moved in.

To my rescue...
My Daddy's loving arms, wide as the ocean,
lifting me above the capsized boats.
He gave me financial literacy
and insights in picking friends.
He inspired me to vote.

To my rescue...
The Love of my Sisterhood/family, friends,
the children sent by God.
My God-links and my Godmother, E. Wong,
rescued me from my loving,
yet mentally ill mother.
"Stella" appeared sweet
in her insanity, but she couldn't be a trusted friend.
I learned to trust myself first,
to be my own ally and confidante.

Rescued by mentors, like Lola, Lissa and Theodosia!
Guided by the ancients and love of children.
Now my mother's clarity is known in dream visits.
I have a Spirit posse traveling with me.

They come to the rescue
of my Goddaughter, Madison.
They protect Madison in the dark,
my mother, father and Mama Byars.

Charles comes to my rescue now.
Making my heaven on earth with thee forever.
He's my partner and travel companion.
Whenever I trip or stumble, he catches me.
He cradles me in his arms. He won't let me fall.

Love is always my refuge. It can be hurdles and leaps of faith.
Balance is knowing the miracles in mistakes.
Understanding the Blessings in broken promises,
the magic in delays, the strength in the climb uphill.
Rescues are growth navigators,
Healing opportunities and blessings.
The rescues strengthen wings to fly,
with courage they fortify Big Mama's kitchen
Our saviors start in the mirror and
build from the inside.

The unseen strengthens us
through people who Love us.
That should make us smile.

Longing

Longing to remember
those moments of clarity
when she laughed and danced around
the house: my mother, when she was
married to my father, it was happy times.
Her eyes were bright, her joy contagious.
My mother was so peaceful before
she became paranoid schizophrenic.
I long for the memory of her loving embrace.
When her mind was clear thinking,
before she descended in to a world of
living, not knowing, not having control of
her mind and weak reality filters.
What a thought. Learning to trust what you
have not, a mother whose mind doesn't
float around and hear voices.
Now, on the other side of the veil
I feel her presence, protecting me
gaining clarity.
She may have lost custody of her four children
to my father when I was ten, but looking back,
she was the best mother I could have.
After more than six decades,
as her namesake daughter,
Stella, I understand unconditional loving.
Love for her grows stronger to this day.
My Pain became Pretty.
The longing became knowing, trusting
and accepting what was, is the best memory
after all.

Meharry Medical College
Nashville, Tennessee

hereby confers upon

Stella S. Wilhite

the degree of

Bachelor of Science in Nursing

together with all the rights, privileges and honors appertaining thereto in consideration of the satisfactory completion of the course prescribed in

The School of Nursing

In Testimony Whereof, the seal of the College and the signatures as authorized by the Board of Trustees are hereunto affixed.

Given at Nashville, on the twentieth day of September, in the year of our Lord nineteen hundred fifty-six.

Chairman of the Board of Trustees
President of the College
Dean of the School of Nursing

Big Mama's Kitchen

Folks are prepping in Big Mama's kitchen. The Duke is at the long table orchestrating the blues. He just got off the "A train" with some bad news.

Queens Ella and Aretha scatting new tunes for Cousin Billie's, "Strange Fruit" salute.

Uncle Martin and Bro. Malcolm adding logs to the fire exchanging tactical moves for the grassroots phase of Black Lives Matters.

Auntie Zora and Uncle Langston are collaborating in the breakfast nook, writing more soul liberation poetry for the days ahead. They say liberation poems are liberation politics. They say victories won with shared ingenuity heal communities.

All gather for another wake this day.

Big Floyd is making his way. A recent addition to the holy gates. On the soul train line he called out for his Mama. Healing for the world came in unexpected ways. Village midwives say the wounds stay open until communities feel safe. They're timing the labor pains.

On the fire, Sistah Fannie Lou is stirring up her sweet potato stew, can't believe fat is this greasy and the eagle didn't fly on Friday so Saturday the children couldn't go out to play. She made peach cobbler and warmed up the fire so they wouldn't feel so cold and bothered awaiting better days.

Prince is on a stool in the corner tuning his guitar in the glow of purple rain. Auntie Maya and Cousin Lucille remind folks Sundays ain't the only day to kneel down and pray.

By the oven, Auntie Shirley talking about voting rights, Sisters Mary McCloud and Mary Beatrice talking about freeing the body and mind. Sister Mary Beatrice Kenner would rest better if more women knew she created the first holder for the sanitary napkin. She was a freshman at Howard University. She fought for the patent for many years! Even her tenacity makes her great. Uncle Nelson cutting up onions and sharpening opinions, planning and plotting for the children's sake. Uncle Marcus slicing carrots while critiquing capitalism's fate. Said it was founded on the slave trade. Both say it grows hollowed souls. They claim human worth is not expendable on any day.

Miss Winnie hugs Uncle Nelson reminding him African queens once led the way.

Once again, wise women are "rising in power" she says.

The stew is on the table!

Bow your heads to each other and the Soul Source provider.

Now it's time to pray.

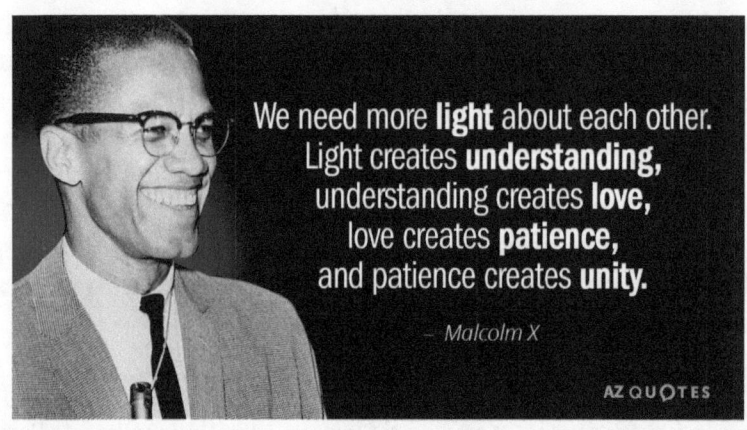

Whole Life Support

Support me in the silence.
Eyes closed with a Maroon Moon night,
darkness brings light.
Unseen, I am still present.
Support me for how I came,
not the way I left,
only my body is absent.
It's a new beginning, no death.

Whole life support is not CPR,
a ventilator or an emergency rescue.
It's the next full breath on any side.
It's love, as the medicine for life,
as jewelry and facets for healing.
Whole life support is knowing life
was there before a body.
It began with the thought of existence, the sacred Yes.
Love can't end. It lives beyond physical boundaries.
Scientifically, matter just changes form. It's Divine Order.
Love always wins. Trust and continue to breathe in life.
Do you remember not ever being here?
The Presence Is the Silence....

The presence is in the Air.

One Nation

Is this country divided?
Ever heard of segregation, Jim Crow
"Separate but equal?"

This country has always been
divided but the percentage is
changing.

Most Black people never agreed with slavery.
Indigenous People never wanted to be slaughtered.
America was built on division and genocide but
"One Nation under God" is in the pledge of Allegiance.
America just needs to have an honest
conversation with itself in the mirror.

I see it this way.

Division starts with a fractured whole.
Wholeness is the focus, there is only
One earth, one nation cradling human civilization.

When there's an earthquake in Morocco or California,
a flood in Libya, tropical storms in Florida, nuclear waste from
Japan
floating in the Pacific Ocean,
we know the oneness of pain, fret and worry.
Americans feel in unison when there's yet
another mass shooting, when people are
invaded in their own country,

when planes hit New York's Twin Towers,
when mothers cry out for their stolen children.

It's one planet when the climate changes,
when a country's democracy is threatened,
when humans are disconnected from each other,
when there's an end to truth
promoted by artificial intelligence.

So when it's said America is divided,
I speak my dreams, my truth into existence.

Say, there may be a decline in racist tendencies.
 Just the last die-hards are the most ambiguous.
Afterall, we had a two-term Black man as
a United States president.
The white extremists do not represent this nation.
Don't let them take the lead on progress.

Say, police abuse is now on body cameras and
Black Lives Matter Grassroots is deeply entrenched.
Police associations are being reviewed and abolished.
The suicide rate of police officers
is the highest among all professions.
Police are more likely to die from self-inflicted bullets.
It's a fact that can't be disputed. Their unions are not
serving them, false pride is hurting their progress.

Change in America came when on
January 6, 2021 Donald Trump's former vice president
Mike Pence was the target of a public lynching!

Anything divided knows how it feels to be fractured but can America practice wholeness without inflicting pain?
A half full glass is my perspective with the rest of the glass filled with hot air and liquid rising.
I see possibilities.
I see one race of human beings getting kinder.
I see Wholeness and healing.
I see division turning to unity.
I pray to the Uniting Force, the Source energy of goodness and Love.
I pray knowing one nation under God indivisible is America's potential.
The U.S. means US.

Hate

Hate is not a healer.
It may feel good but it's a temporary remedy.
It may feel justified but it's a heavy load
to carry shadows into the future.
It may fill you up temporarily with satisfaction,
but it crowds out loving.

Hate is the weapon that has no friends.
It's incapable of compassion, understanding and lessons.
And it has a hidden target. It has a reciprocal nature.

It can't see beauty in the mirror. It's blind to inner peace.
It uses weapons of self-alienation.
Hate can't be a healer because it runs
 joy out of town even in the hereafter!

Hell is hate and revenge is an overcrowded prison.

The Origin Story

Broken parts come from Wholeness.
Sometimes a broken heart can't stop
destiny revealed in fractured parts.

But...doesn't Wholeness have memory
in fractured form? Wholeness was the beginning.
Can memories, thought heroically, help the wounds to heal?

Maybe it's not broken but re-purposed
or re-engineered as reminders nothing is ever lost or fractured.
Everything just has its time and place.

Sometimes the last sound of completeness/
of fullness/of wholeness is silence.
Impermanence helps the broken disappear.

What is the fractured value when returning to its origins?
What do the broken parts reveal?

I Asked the Border Patrol,
"Aren't They Human?"

I ask the border patrolman,
"aren't they human?"
Would you want to be treated
like cattle, like your life doesn't matter?
How can another human being,
from a United States agency,
roundup people like animals on horseback?

I ask the refugee, the wanderer,
the children running from hell and horror,
what are your dreams, what is your heaven?
Is safety your joy? Can my prayers help you?

I ask our neighbors, the community,
the gathering of politicians for elections,
on the streets when will we see the homeless
when will seniors and children be cared for?
How do we decrease populations of the poor?
In the mirror, I ask what can you do
to expand the hearts of human beings?

The answers are the reflections of those
absorbed by fear and insecurities.

"They are just not producing."
"Yes, but," is their answer.
Everyman for herself is his training.
Division and "other" their weapon.
Yes, but, no is their behavior.

No help for the destitute,
the hopeless,
those who feel betrayed, who live
in mental crisis and American veterans
living under highways.
Can we just offer some options
is my request. This is a question
to anyone who reads this.
I am the daughter of a proud
Korean POW veteran. A purple
Heart recipient.
He believed in this country.

So I just keep writing.

Maybe poets can help.

Why Old Loves Died Young

Memories linger long enough to ponder...
Why old Loves became the dearly departed so early.
Why did old loves leave so soon?
Why did overripe fruit attract flies?
Why did crackers grow stale?
Why did cupboards go bare?
Why did the dance music become
noise and senseless chatter?
Old loves died young, because
friendship was never the foundation.
We blamed each other for what
we lacked.   Instead of working on ourselves
we wanted to change each other.

Learning how to be the love of my life was
when the Old Loves started dying younger and younger.

EACH death was more than a cry, it was a wink,
It was the Divine's perfect timing!

Madison's Gigi (2021)

A child's life held in sacred arms.
Her spirit of Light lives inside me.
A neighbor whose child I hold dearly.
An ache for her well-being.
How do I strengthen light to endure uncertainty?
Disappearing in a hazy fog of unknowing
she's my grand-Godchild.
The first seven years of her living, I was her "Gigi".

Now she's ten. Her mother has a new boyfriend,
new baby, a different life and interest.
As the sun disappears beyond the horizon
hellos and goodbyes are left empty. I dream of her.
I cloak her in love and peace as protection.
As the light hides behind thick clouds
the emergence of her star's radiance is forever.

It's unfair to feel lost as a faith-walker,
But sometimes...I do.

A Better Understanding

It was in my mother's bathroom,
thoughts of dread.
My fate and future looked dim,
choices felt limited
love not found anywhere.

Chaos, confusion,
conflicting emotions in my head.
A ten-year-old's nightmare,
a life in the hands of
a schizophrenic mother
who couldn't trust herself or anybody else.
It was the mix of toilet bowl cleaner
and the rubbing alcohol,
the warning on the label,
"keep out of the reach of children",
when I turned the glass up.
Woke up in the dark, with a light
above my head.
It was the hospital room,
stomach pumped. To tell this
story, I needed to live.
Survival is knowing there's something greater.
My creator was there to tell me it's not over.
There is something greater than my thoughts.
A dominion of loving grace is
my happy ever-after.
Grateful for the light
when I opened my eyes finally.

Grateful for the gift of each day
my Inner Being held me.
The light is my sanctuary.
It has never been pitch
black since
that day I was ten.
Still here to love me again and again.
More than fifty years later,
Grateful to the Light that rescued
a child who didn't feel willing or able.

Why the Weeping Willow Weeps

The weeping willow weeps for humanity.
The tears soften the edges of chaos and catastrophes.
The willow weeps for the shocked, displaced,
disheartened human beings trying to find their way.
The willow weeps for all God's children.
It's a future that's hard to see.
The willow weeps for the forgotten,
the abused, suicidal pleas,
the willow weeps for the earth,
the air, for those who love and care...
the willow is rooted in its wish for me.
Its tears water seeds for victories
not yet seen. Tears grieving genocides,
victims, the innocent, collateral damage, emotional zombies.
Tears of compassion and empathy
for the homeless, war-torn cities and refugees.
It weeps for the tears stuck in
throats of souls who couldn't flee.
The weeping willow is rooted in love
watered by tears as it, too, keeps growing.

Enough Already

You want to be right?
You want to be Far Right???

Then right some wrongs from far too long.
Enough making mass shootings
routine in America!

Enough Already!

Enslavement

Four-hundred-years and counting.
With the growth of private penitentiaries
you enslave.
You take human dignity away.
You take identity, culture, education,
parents, children away. You lock people in cages.
You take languages and names.
And you ask that I not rage?
You ask that I not raise my voice to a shout?
You insist the tears are temporary?
Racism has confused Ken and Barbie.
You enslave and then have
selective memory.
You're responsible for
the genocide of native Americans and put Africans in bondage.
You ask me not to rage? Do you see your history?
What about reparations? Maybe its time to look in the mirror?
What happened to liberty and justice for all? Is it a just a mirage?

"Senufo Sculpture by Charles Dickson", materials, stainless Steel

Dick and Jane

Dick and Jane readers hindsight is 2020. This is a rewrite for the new first graders.

See Jane run. Jane runs after Dick.
Dick is slick. Jane has no fun in the sun with Dick.
But Jane and Dick have lots of tricks.
Jane loves Dick.
She has no fun, but Jane never quits.
She knows Dick is slick.
Dick and Jane's power is mixed.
They taught me to read in the first grade.
I learned to read between the cracks
as their kinfolks broke my mother's back
raped sisters and hung cousins from trees.
Racism, like weeds, grows between white concrete.
But Jane and Dick set me free.
While Dick and Jane never looked like me
played with me or shared possibilities,
learning to read was my remedy.
Dick was a prick Jane couldn't fix.
She's learning new tricks and finding new friends to play with.

"See Jane Run"

Emotional Baggage

Emotional baggage...
Its holder, its carrier,
burdens held hostage are heavy loads.
Backpacks make chronic hunched backs,
they carry the freedom of travel but it's slow.
Baggage is home with glued on bandages,
wounds never addressed or healed.
Shadows hugging light.
Views offered from prisons,
special keys made for locked doors.
Limp bodies, feel the soul's absence,
a refuge, voids, judgement without a cause.
New day, if desired, baggage unpacked.
Download worries and troubles. Promises of
brighter days ahead. A new survey.
What is carried that's not needed anymore?
In this now, what purpose does it serve?
Moving forward means not looking back.
Feelings are uncomfortable, even sad.
But they're not bad, they're just unpleasant.
Ride the wave, lean into them for sixty-to-ninety seconds.
New insights appear on the other side.
To release pain, you have to get close enough to touch it,
unlike fire, it won't scorch you, just warm you, I promise.
When ears can see, eyes can hear, hearts open.
Discernment comes with discretion. That's wisdom.
Become Lighter than a feather
without a carrier. Galaxy Flight options.
You're the pilot, private jet, but no baggage allowed.

You're the carrier. Examine the weight.
What lie do you believe about the world,
yourself or others.
Is the world fair? No.
Fairness has nothing to do with your
arrival or departure.
But does the Creator provide balance? Yes.
For flights of joy, happiness and peaceful
coexistence, unload your backpack.
Next time you look in the mirror,
ask this question...
What's holding you back?
What lie is keeping your pain intact?

Your answer will change everything.

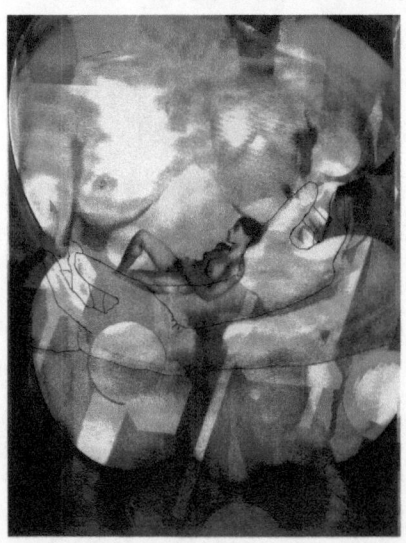

"Photo Alchemy", by Charles Dickson

I Know New

I remember getting my first glimpse of her.
I knew New when she walked in the door
I knew New when she didn't mind
telling folks the truth anymore.
I knew New when she told him
his screwing around wasn't new
but the new screw she knew
and New doesn't live in secret anymore.
I knew New when she hung up the phone.
New became my new best friend,
we hang out more and more.
Knew New something needed to change.
Looking forward means refraining from passing blame.
New means new directions.
These days New doesn't take chances.
New Life lessons are important to
hold close and learn.

Shadows Covering Light

Dark days are here,
"shadows covering light,"
says tv reporter, Rachel Maddow.
If you're wondering if
democracy can be dismantled, the answer is yes.
It's being shredded to the bone by Trumpism.
Yes, deal in the Light, the darkside says,
"give them childn' s some shortening bread".
Shortin' their lives with stressful tweets,
shortin' their lives with counterfeit meat.
Shortin' their lives with air they can't breathe,
water they can't drink, shortin their lives
with covid-19. Shortin' their lives by power and greed.
Lying, manipulating, corrupting and destroying the people.
What a time to live in this land!
High ground is the only ground, the rest in quicksand.
We the People, empowered, we stand.
20/20 is balanced vision...
Now is the time to see the impact of your decisions!
America has karma.... Hope that makes you smile and proud
to serve an America still looking for its greatness.

Upper Limits, Hidden Flaws

Upper limits, hidden flaws
Surprise reactions the self can't
point to the cause.
It was buried a long time ago
unaware you carry such a heavy load.

Upper limit, hidden flaws
Know the cause of your faltering,
the conditions in your self-loving
Upper limits reveal upper flaws.
To dissolve, make space
for flaws dissolving.
It's no longer important to disguise the cause.
Maybe the reason you have the pain
is so you can dig up the seeds to thaw.
Pain was buried with the seeds, that's the cause
No flaw in the seeds it's just the need to thaw them.
Close to the core, pain so deep the work
is knowing it was never yours to keep.

Learning to be Grateful

Grateful to know love of community
mourning together when
the innocent and children are slaughtered.

Grateful to trust, with fear
at bay, when tears flow through
cracks and grooves
in sacred paths and winding highways.

Grateful to be Black knowing
"whiteness" is an artificial construct,
an identity whose power fears the sun.

Grateful to know self-forgiveness
and Light moving in mysterious ways.
Love, Magic & Maroon Moons
is nurturing food on hungry days,
filling my life with grace and acceptance.

Grateful to feel humanity
in a group of poets
intuitively having their say.

Grateful to know there's a higher power
taking care of human beings, praising peace
pushing through problems,
peeling away doubt
loving and knowing,
Love has the final word each day.

That's how I sleep, that's how I wake.

This is a prayerful poem to get me through
the 21st Century!
We heal in community, listening is how
we serve each other.
Grateful to share these words.

Acknowledgments

Love. Love for writing, love for people, love for a country and an earth that was made beautiful from birth. I am so grateful for the love of my friends and family who make this book and my living so much easier.

The title starts with Love. Love for my friend/partner, artist extraordinaire, Charles Dickson, who had to hear so many of these poems, so many times. I am sure his favorite ones are the ones he inspired. His brilliance as a sculptor and multidisciplinary artist more than thirty years ago created a resonance between us lasting to this day.

To God be the Glory! Love pours in us, all needs are met. In an attempt to name a few folks for seeing me and/or this book to the finish line, I am grateful for my Godmother, Evelyn Wong Hemsley, who believes always that I can do whatever I put my mind to accomplish and do it well. She is my first proofreader, editor, confidante, advisor and wisdom keeper. We have a Love like no other. No question, God sent her here. She's an exceptional human being who at 92 still likes to curse and raise hell if necessary. She's my rock and soft place to land. E. Wong knows my heart and we can read each other's minds. She still recites poetry from childhood memories.

Eileen Cohen, my editor, serious proofreader, client and dear friend. She has taught me so much about honoring my voice, and second guessing myself. She has supported this work and my life's work for more than two decades. She offered to edit the first book of poetry, and she brings her insights to this one as well. Her insistence on getting it right, teaches me the importance of every single period, comma, semicolon and paragraph edits. Most of all, she helps me understand to allow my words to flow. Love, Magic & Maroon Moons is an act of Love and Magic. It's the "Maroon Moons" in
life giving birth to this second poetry series. I am so grateful to my dear friend, Phoebe Beasley, a famous and fabulous artist and friend. Her artwork, Maroon Moon inspired the title of this book.

I have so many dear friends and family members who simply stick by me. From my cousin Lydia Thomas and my sistahs, Denise Wheatley Rowe, Janice Marshall, Karen Waters, Ann Curry, Rickie Byars, Georgia Anne Muldrow, Patricia Ann Smith, Ashley Wilkerson, Eisha Mason, Greta Sesheta, Tracy Jones, Brenda Jones, Dorothy Randall Gray and the International Women's Writing Guild.

And so many others, have always encouraged me to use my voice including my Instagram friends (@stella the poet). You have been instrumental in how I have expressed myself authentically as a writer. You have supported poetry readings and events where literary arts are showcased. Thank You!

Grateful to Hiram Sims and everyone at World Stage Press, Chaeyeon Park, Sage Herrin and Jessica Lin at the Community Literature Initiative who made this book possible. It's a blessing to be able to work with you.

To my Godchildren, from Hadiya & Eric Ellis (Faruq & Cire), Amber Witcher, Quia and Titiana, Madison Theus, plus, plus.... my life is good because you help to fuel the love in it.

Thank you to ascended masters, teachers, guides and guardians, my mother and father, grandparents, Alica Ligon Holeman and Louise Wilhite. I feel you daily.

Much Love to ALL named and unnamed sources making life possible and loving us along the way!

Photography Credits

Barbara Lynn Parker - Moonlights, Sunsets, Lightning, Instagram: @Barbarellax3
barbara.parker1@outlook.com

Evelyn Wong Hemsley - Family vintage photos including yearbook staff 1930, Bethune Cookman College, Evelyn Wong with her brothers, "One Nation", family photo with grandfather, Lamar Williams and her mother and aunts, "My Style" at her wedding to Hubert Hemsley with her sister-in-laws on her wedding day. "A Blessing of Thanksgiving" bathing suit queens on the cover of Ebony Magazine in the 1950s for Bethune Cookman college, Evelyn Hemsley and friends.

Stella Wilhite - maternal family photos on the poem, 94% Strong. Family album including but not limited to graduation cap and gown from Meharry Medical College, her mother Louise Wilhite on the last page.

Hadiya Walter and Eric Ellis are the photographers of family fotos on the poems "Loving is a Verb," "When Love Calls," and collage on page 7.

Estella Holeman - Family photos including niece and nephew, Robert Holeman III and Taylor Holeman, photos also courtesy of Robert L. Holeman, husband of Stella Holeman, "Be Kind" with Janice Marshall in South Africa

Charles Dickson - Public Art photos of "Wishing on a Star" in front of the California African American Museum in Los Angeles. Photo alchemy of pregnant woman on "Unspoken". Senufo heads with the poem, "Enslavement" and a bronze heart with the poem, "the Origin Story". "Photo Alchemy" with the poem "Emotional Baggage". "Surrender" hand-carved acrylic on "My Wingspan."...Instagram:
@dicksonstudio4233 and www.thedicksonstudio.com

Grandmommy Louise

Publisher's Note

Daxson publishing was created to help marginalized artists and their allies publish their work, so the world can hear their voice. The vision for this publishing house is to help people get their work out there, and not have them struggle finding their way through the publishing process. Everyone's voice deserves to be heard, and we are here to help. If you are interested in submitting a manuscript, email daxsonpublishing@gmail.com. Support our cause! Buy our books at daxsonpublishing.com.

www.ingramcontent.com/pod-product-compliance
Lightning Source LLC
LaVergne TN
LVHW040103080526
838202LV00045B/3760